TOWN DOG

Carolyn Bear

Illustrated by
Scoular Anderson

OXFORD
UNIVERSITY PRESS

UNIVERSITY PRESS

Great Clarendon Street, Oxford OX2 6DP

Oxford University Press is a department of the University of Oxford.
It furthers the University's objective of excellence in research, scholarship,
and education by publishing worldwide in

Oxford New York

Auckland Cape Town Dar es Salaam Hong Kong Karachi
Kuala Lumpur Madrid Melbourne Mexico City Nairobi
New Delhi Shanghai Taipei Toronto

With offices in

Argentina Austria Brazil Chile Czech Republic France Greece
Guatemala Hungary Italy Japan South Korea Poland Portugal
Singapore Switzerland Thailand Turkey Ukraine Vietnam

Oxford is a registered trade mark of Oxford University Press
in the UK and in certain other countries

British Library Cataloguing in Publication Data

Data available

ISBN-10: 0-19-919597-8
ISBN-13: 978-0-19-919597-8

5 7 9 10 8 6

Mixed Pack (1 of 6 different titles): ISBN 0 19 919601 X
Class Pack (6 copies of 6 titles): ISBN 0 19 919600 1

Printed in China by Imago

Contents

Chapter 1
Clever Dog

The Town Dog lived with a Little Old Lady.

The Little Old Lady loved her. She let her sleep on her bed and sit on her lap like a cat.

The Town Dog, whose name was
Lou-Lou, had a coat to wear when
it was cold.

And when it rained the Little Old
Lady let her ride in her shopping trolley.
Lou-Lou liked to hide in the trolley.

Then she would pop out from under
the shopping and make people jump.

Lou-Lou was a very clever dog. She
had some important jobs to do.

She had to bark when the Little Old
Lady didn't hear the doorbell.

She had to warn the Little Old
Lady when something was burning
in the kitchen.

And she had to clean up any food
that fell on the floor.

When the Little Old Lady lost
things, like her keys or her purse,
all she had to do was say "keys"
or "purse" and Lou-Lou would run
and find them.

Then the Little Old Lady would
give her treats.

Lou-Lou really was the happiest dog
in the world.

One day something terrible
happened. The Little Old Lady had a
fall and broke her leg and was carried
off to hospital. Lou-Lou wasn't allowed
to go in the ambulance with her.

She was left all alone in the house with a dish of food and a bowl of water. She couldn't sleep all night. And she didn't eat the food. She was very sad and very worried.

She thought she would never see the Little Old Lady again.

Chapter Two

Lou-Lou's New Home

The next day, a man in a uniform came and opened the front door without even ringing the doorbell. He had a cap with a badge with the letters R.S.P.C.A. on it.

Lou-Lou barked and barked. She even growled – which surprised her. It was something she didn't know she could do.

He put Lou-Lou in a basket and carried her out to a van. She whined and scratched at the basket. Was she being kidnapped?

But the man took her to a train station. Then he put her on a train with lots of parcels and sacks and bicycles. Doors slammed and the train started off.

Lou-Lou's basket rocked in time
with the train. *Dig-a-dig-rick,
dig-a-dig-rick, rick-a-rick-rick-rick,
duggedy-duggedy-duggedy.*

Lou-Lou whimpered miserably. But
no one came. At last she dropped off
to sleep.

The next thing she knew, the train
had stopped.

Her basket was lifted up and carried
out of the train.

She sniffed the air. It didn't smell
at all like the town. There were
interesting animal smells and strange,
scary smells she'd never smelt before.

Her basket was handed to a man
who was waiting on the platform. He
was wearing wellies covered with
mud. Lou Lou crouched down in her
basket with her ears back. Where was
he taking her?

He put the basket in the back of a car. There was a woman in the front and a Terrible Child strapped into a baby-seat in the back.

The Terrible Child was screaming and the woman was trying to make it quiet by waving a toy at it.

Further back, behind bars, there
were two huge and fierce-looking dogs.
They barked at Lou-Lou with deep,
hollow barks.

The Terrible Child stopped crying
when he saw Lou-Lou. He poked his
hand into her basket and tried to pull
her tail.

After a long and bumpy journey,
they arrived at a farm. The man and
the woman climbed out of the car.
They took the Terrible Child out of the
baby-seat and opened the back of the
car to let out the big dogs.

Then they opened Lou-Lou's basket
and said, "Out you get."

Lou-Lou jumped out straight into
a puddle. Rain was soaking through
her fur and the wind was icy. She had
to walk along a horrible, muddy track
with the other dogs.

Lou-Lou walked on tip-toe and
jumped over the puddles. The other
dogs didn't mind getting wet and dirty
and they barked at Lou-Lou in a
jeering way.

When they reached the house, all
the dogs were taken into a back room
with a cold stone floor and given bowls
of dog food.

There were two cats there, too, and
they came and sniffed Lou-Lou, to find
out if she was a cat.

Lou-Lou barked to make sure they
knew she was a dog. They backed away
and Lou-Lou was glad.

Lou-Lou was very hungry, but she
didn't eat her dinner. She jumped back
into her basket and tried to go to sleep.

It was a freezing night, and very
dark outside. And animals she didn't
know made strange and frightening
noises. The other two dogs slept on the
stone floor and snored and didn't seem
to care.

Lou-Lou lay awake thinking of the saucer of hot cocoa and the biscuit that she used to have at home with the Little Old Lady.

When at last she fell asleep, she dreamed she was riding in a shopping trolley full of big, juicy bones.

Chapter Three

Lou-Lou in Disgrace

The next day, the man came in wearing his wellies. He took the other two dogs with him and went out into the fields.

That's when Lou-Lou heard this terrible "BANG!" outside. It was followed by a lot more even louder BANGS!

Lou-Lou was so frightened she
buried herself in a basket of washing.
When the woman came to do the
ironing, she found her. She was
really angry.

So Lou-Lou was in disgrace. She sat
quietly in a corner and watched the
Terrible Child.

The Terrible Child threw a lot of
food and toys around and then he
went to sleep. When he woke up
again, he threw a lot more food and
then he started chasing Lou-Lou round
the room.

That's when she discovered that she
could jump out through the cat flap.

That night, the two dogs came back
with the man. They had a big sack full
of dead birds with them.

The two dogs were covered with
mud and smelled as if they had rolled
in something horrible. They growled at
Lou-Lou and she tried to get as far
away from them as she could.

26

She jumped onto the woman's lap.
The woman wasn't a bit like the Little
Old Lady. She pushed Lou-Lou off.

Then the man said he was going to
teach Lou-Lou how to behave like a
proper dog.

Chapter Four
Lucky Escape

For the next week, Lou-Lou had a terrible time. She didn't want to learn how to behave like a dog. For a start, she had to spend all day outside, even when it was raining. Her tail was down and her ears were back all the time.

The other dogs just laughed at her
and showed off. They didn't want to
play with her.

There were some huge animals in
the fields that she hadn't seen before.
At first, Lou-Lou thought they were
dogs. But they didn't smell like dogs
and they didn't bark.

She went to take a closer look. One
of them was bigger than the others.
When he saw Lou-Lou he rolled his
eyes and snorted.

He had huge sharp horns. He
lowered his head and pawed the
ground. It was a bull.

Lou-Lou started backing away. Then she started running. She could hear the bull thundering after her. She ran as fast as her four legs would take her.

She shot through a gap in the hedge just as the bull was about to toss her in the air.

After that, Lou-Lou decided it would
be best to play with smaller animals.
She even tried to make friends with
the cats. One of their favourite games
was chasing each other round the
house and garden in and out through
the cat flap. Lou-Lou joined in.

The two big dogs looked on in disgust.

"A dog going through a cat flap," said one of them, and laughed in a nasty way. And the other dog sniggered. Lou-Lou felt very ashamed.

Chapter Five

To the Rescue

Then, early one morning, the woman took the man to catch the train. Lou-Lou was sitting in the back of the car. She wondered where he was going.

When the woman got back she started to clean the whole house.

When she had finished cleaning,
she set the table with a tablecloth and
the best china.

The dogs were told to stay outside
so that they didn't make muddy
pawprints everywhere.

But Lou-Lou crept in through the
cat flap. She hid under the table.

Lou-Lou watched as the woman got the Terrible Child ready in his outdoor clothes. Then the woman took a rug out to the car.

But the minute that she was outside, the Terrible Child toddled across the floor and slammed the front door shut. Lou-Lou was locked in – and so was the Terrible Child!

The Terrible Child then walked over
to the table and pulled at the
tablecloth.

All the tea cups and saucers and
plates and spoons and jam and milk
went sliding with a terrible crash onto
the floor. Lou-Lou was shocked.

The woman was now peering
through the letterbox.

She called out, "Don't do that!
Come to Mummy."

But the Terrible Child took no
notice. He went over to the fireplace
and started throwing things into
the fire.

A magazine slid out of the fire on to
the rug. A thin wisp of flame started to
dart across the floor.

The woman was screaming. She was
desperate. She could see her keys on
the table, but couldn't get to them.

"Keys," she shouted to the Terrible
Child. "Bring the keys to Mummy."

Lou-Lou pricked up her ears. "Keys!"

The Terrible Child didn't understand.
The other two dogs stared through the
window helplessly. The cats were
trying to climb up the curtains.

All the animals were terrified.
They didn't know what to do.

Lou-Lou spotted the keys lying on
the table. Quick as a flash, she jumped
up on a chair and grasped the keys in
her mouth. Then she dashed out
through the cat flap. She gave the keys
to the woman.

The woman unlocked the door,
raced into the room and threw the rug
over the flames, and put them out.
She picked up the Terrible Child and
hugged him. She was crying. Then she
turned to Lou-Lou.

"Oh, you good dog," she said,
blowing her nose.

"What a clever dog you are," she
said, wiping her eyes. And she lifted
Lou-Lou up and hugged her too.

The other dogs looked at Lou-Lou
with respect.

Lou-Lou felt so proud.

Chapter Six
Home Again

The woman made sure that the fire was well and truly out and cleared up the mess on the floor. Then she bundled the Terrible Child and Lou-Lou into the car and drove off at a very fast pace.

The Terrible Child was quiet for once. He stroked Lou-Lou nicely and said "Doc-Duc," which was the nearest he could get to "Good dog."

Soon they arrived at the train
station. The woman got out of the car
and she took the Terrible Child and
Lou-Lou with her.

They went onto the platform
and waited for the train to come.
Lou-Lou expected they were waiting
for the man.

And sure enough, as the train came
in, there he was, waving through the
window.

He climbed out of the train. And
then a guard came and helped him
carry something heavy out of the train.
It was a wheelchair and sitting in it,
who should it be but the Little Old
Lady, with her leg all done up in a big
plaster cast!

Lou-Lou went almost mad with joy.
She leapt up and tried to lick the Little
Old Lady's face.

Then the woman told the man how
clever Lou-Lou had been. After that,
she was allowed to ride back home on
the Little Old Lady's lap.

Lou-Lou stayed in the country until
the Little Old Lady's leg got better.

While they were in the country, nobody tried to make her behave like a dog any more. They let her stay inside in the warm and sit with the Little Old Lady.

The other dogs didn't laugh or snigger at her, either. They looked up to her with respect.

About the author

The idea for writing this book came from a real dog. Her owner couldn't look after her any more in the city, so she came to live with us in the country.

The first time she saw a cow she came back through the hedge with her eyes as big as saucers. She wouldn't go out in the rain and used to tip-toe round the puddles. But she's a very intelligent dog. And, with time, she's got used to country life. She's sitting beside me now and looks as if she'd like to add a word or two herself if only she could type.

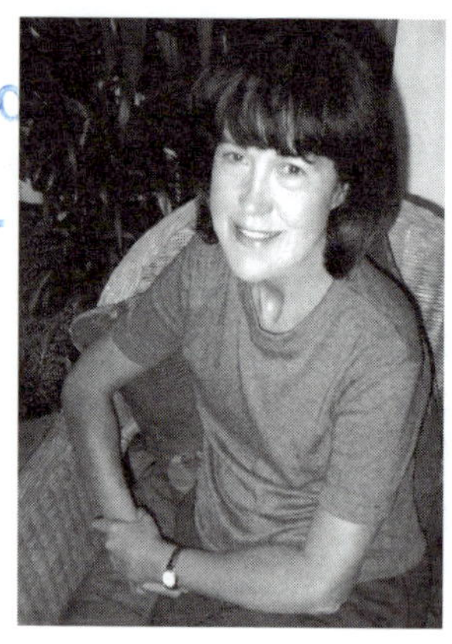